BEIJING
THE CITY AT A GLANCE

GW00836239

Jingshan Park
Climb the manmade hill in this popu[
once an imperial garden, for sweepi[
Jingshan Qianjie

Galaxy Soho
Zaha Hadid's mall has split opinion, winning
architectural awards while facing criticism
from local heritage groups – judge for yourself.
See p080

Forbidden City
The last emperor left in 1924, leaving 8,700
rooms in mothballs. Thanks to the Olympics and
restorers, more areas are now open to view.
See p012

CCTV Building
Despite the best intentions of the architects,
this CBD landmark has been beset by problems.
See p010

China World Trade Center Tower III
Wait for a clear day to visit the Shangri-La's
80th-floor Atmosphere bar (T 6505 6432).
See p009

Beijing Railway Station
Its 1959 facade belies advances made by the
Chinese rail system. The world's longest high-
speed network has 11,000km of track already.
See p080

National Museum of China
This vast exhibition space reopened in 2011, its
collection numbering more than 1m artefacts.
16 Dongchang'an Jie, T 6511 6400

NCPA
Paul Andreu's once-divisive design has proved
to be a boon for the performing arts.
See p084

INTRODUCTION
THE CHANGING FACE OF THE URBAN SCENE

Beijing is, without doubt, one of the world's fastest-changing cities. A generation-defining transformation is underway, one that shifted to warp speed in the run-up to the 2008 Olympics, and the zeal to modernise has continued apace long after the circus moved on. There is a growing assertiveness in Chinese politics, culture and economics. Yet its roaring cities and high-flying corporations belie a far messier underbelly – from the debt bubbles of the construction boom to an insatiable need for energy, and the choking pollution and toxic haze – all of which is not lost on an unruly netizenry, and a government painfully trying to chart a more sustainable future.

China's capital lies at the beating heart of this complex beast. Sure, its southern rival Shanghai may be the glitzy financial hub, but there's something addictive about Beijing. Smooth or pretty it ain't, but this epicentre of undiluted political power is also home to a rich culture and a monumental spirit, from the imperial grandeur to cutting-edge contemporary architecture. Just as the city boggles the mind with its many contradictions, it remains a bubbling hotpot of possibilities. This is where all the major decisions get made and big business gets done. Although frustrations do exist, particularly when the powers that be enact one of their sporadic clampdowns, the capital is ultimately where this huge country's most talented artists and designers are drawn for inspiration, by the impalpable but very real feeling that here, today, something is happening.

ESSENTIAL INFO
FACTS, FIGURES AND USEFUL ADDRESSES

TOURIST OFFICE
269 Wangfujing Dajie
T 8511 3533
www.visitbeijing.com.cn

TRANSPORT
Airport transfer
The Airport Express takes 35 minutes to Beijing Dongzhimen (RMB25). The service runs from 6.20am until 11.10pm
Car hire
China Auto Rental
T 5820 9999
www.zuche.com
Public transport
The subway runs from 5am until 11pm
www.bjsubway.com
Taxis
Beijing Taxi Dispatch Centre
T 6837 3366
Cabs can also be hailed on the street

EMERGENCY SERVICES
Ambulance
T 120
Fire
T 119
Police
T 110
24-hour pharmacy
Suite 105
Wing 1
Kunsha Dasha
16 Xinyuanli
T 6462 9112
www.internationalsos.com

EMBASSIES
British Embassy
11 Guanghua Lu
T 5192 4000
www.ukinchina.fco.gov.uk

US Embassy
55 Anjialou Lu
T 8531 3000
beijing.usembassy-china.org.cn

POSTAL SERVICES
Post office
50 Guanghua Lu
T 6512 8120
Shipping
UPS
3 Zaoying Lu
T 6587 6166

BOOKS
Age of Ambition: Chasing Fortune, Truth and Faith in the New China by Evan Osnos (Bodley Head)
Midnight in Peking by Paul French (Penguin)
Nine Lives: The Birth of Avant-Garde Art in New China by Karen Smith (Timezone 8)

WEBSITES
Art/design
www.design-china.org
www.leapleapleap.com
Newspapers
www.chinadaily.com.cn

COST OF LIVING
Taxi from Beijing Capital International Airport to city centre
RMB100 (including RMB10 toll)
Cappuccino
RMB30
Packet of cigarettes
RMB10
Daily newspaper
RMB1.5
Bottle of champagne
RMB750

BEIJING
Population
21 million
Currency
Renminbi
Telephone codes
China: 86
Beijing: 10
Time
GMT +8
Flight time
London: 10 hrs 30 minutes

Sapporo
Tokyo
Osaka
Beijing
CHINA
Shanghai
Hong Kong
Kolkata

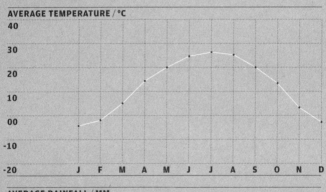

AVERAGE TEMPERATURE / °C

40												
30												
20												
10												
00												
-10												
-20	J	F	M	A	M	J	J	A	S	O	N	D

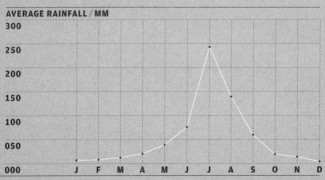

AVERAGE RAINFALL / MM

300												
250												
200												
150												
100												
050												
000	J	F	M	A	M	J	J	A	S	O	N	D

NEIGHBOURHOODS

THE AREAS YOU NEED TO KNOW AND WHY

To help you navigate the city, we've chosen the most interesting districts (see below and the map inside the back cover) and colour-coded our featured venues, according to their location; those venues that are outside these areas are not coloured.

EAST SIDE

OMA's HQ for the state broadcaster, CCTV (see p010), has redrawn the landscape of Beijing's CBD, while construction along the East Third Ring Road continues to yield a mountain range of glass-and-steel skyscrapers. Ghettoes of quietude can be found in the old embassy area, though perhaps not in the Russian neighbourhood around Yabao Lu. Climb the rockery in the perfectly manicured Ritan Park for a great view of Chaoyang business district.

UNIVERSITIES

Liang Sicheng, the founder of China's leading school of architecture at Tsinghua University, begged Mao to save the walls of the old city and build a new administrative centre to its north-west. Alas, he and his Soviet advisers declined. But the digital economy is making up for Mao's miscue. The area is no longer home to punks and poor scholars, but research institutes, internet cafés and towers of tech geeks.

TIANANMEN

The geographical and historical centre of the city is a hopscotch through the yin and yang of modern China's past. Dine at Brian McKenna at The Courtyard (see p045) next to the East Gate of the Forbidden City (see p012), whose doors open daily, unlike those of the adjacent Communist Party HQ. Next to the Great Hall of the People (see p080), a big classical box, is Paul Andreu's NCPA (see p084) – a futuristic bubble.

GULOU

Sadly, a whole chunk of this part of the old city has fallen prey to the wrecking ball and rents have surged throughout many of the hutong, threatening the bohemian equilibrium of the area. But the hipsters remain, as does the abundance of trendy shops, bars and restaurants. The action happens around the Drum and Bell Towers, Nanluoguxiang and Gulou Dongdajie, with many venues, such as Dali Courtyard (see p051), secreted in the alleyways.

OLD CITY

Once home to concubines, warlords and the literati, the labyrinthine blocks surrounding the emperor's old 'hood are prime real estate once again. In the interim, the area was ravaged by Maoist collectivisation and Olympic-driven modernisation. Properties like Hotel Côté Cour (see p022) are hidden gems amid the ersatz malls. Visit the Temple of Heaven (see p033) for imperial-era inspiration.

SANLITUN

The nexus of Beijing nightlife. Expats christened the leafy embassy zone with a few pubs in the early 1990s and beloved hangouts were soon born on Sanlitun Nanlu. Retail complexes such as Taikoo Li, home of shops like Brand New China (see p094), have shifted the area upmarket, limiting the colourful seediness to a single back alley. Clubs and drinking dens still flourish around the Workers' Stadium.

LANDMARKS

THE SHAPE OF THE CITY SKYLINE

Credit the Mongols, who under Kublai Khan founded the Yuan dynasty (1271-1368), for Beijing's masterplan. It called for the 'Great Capital' to be laid out on a symmetrical grid with a central axis that bisects the imperial palace. The early Ming emperors erected the Forbidden City (see p012) at the core, and the Qing dynasty Manchus kept that schema intact. Not so Mao's planners, who tore down the city wall to build the Second Ring Road. This set the pattern of concentric ring roads that has rippled outwards ever since, with a 940km-long Seventh Ring Road currently in the works. Beijing's layout – as incomprehensible as it may appear on the ground – is self-explanatory. The city is its own compass.

Today, the north is best known for the Olympic Green's modern landmarks – the National Stadium (see p014) and the National Aquatics Center (11 Tianchen Donglu, T 8437 0112) – whereas the south is dominated by imperial-era relics (see p033). The east is closest to what could be termed downtown, with a CBD around the CCTV Building (overleaf) and the 330m-high China World Trade Center Tower III (1 Jianguomenwai Dajie, T 6505 2288).

Despite improvements in mobility as the subway is extended, getting around still isn't simple. Kilometre-square blocks make most districts unwalkable, and although taxis are cheap, those riding in them are resigned to serious gridlock during rush hour. *For full addresses, see Resources.*

CCTV Building

Ole Scheeren and Rem Koolhaas' building for China's television network, CCTV, has redefined the look of the fast-rising CBD. There is perhaps no better symbol of the ambition of 21st-century Beijing than this $1.2bn glass-and-steel loop, popularly nicknamed the 'big underpants'. Rather than join the city's unthinking race for the heavens, the structure has two leaning towers – one used for broadcasting, the other for offices – bending at right angles to meet on the ground, and, giddily, at the top. The complex has not been without its problems, albeit through no fault of its own. Engineering firm Arup broke ground in 2004, but it was only finished in 2012, delayed by damage after an unauthorised fireworks display in 2009 engulfed OMA's adjacent cultural centre and hotel tower. This home for the Mandarin Oriental (see p016) should be finally ready in late 2015.
East Third Ring Road/Guanghua Lu

Forbidden City

Chairman Mao faced south, just as any emperor of yore would have done, on declaring his dominion from the Forbidden City's Gate of Heavenly Peace in 1949. His portrait now hangs above the main entrance to this former imperial palace, but superstition, it is said, stopped him ever setting foot inside. The 720,000 sq m complex was commissioned in 1406 and symbolically sits on the city's central axis. Its ornate towers and red-painted walls – their bricks made from white lime and glutinous rice, cemented with mortar containing egg white – sparkle under a blanket of snow or at night, particularly around the ghostly moat (pictured) at the Wumen gate. Inside lie the treasures of the Palace Museum. *North of Tiananmen Square, T 8500 7421, www.dpm.org.cn*

National Stadium

The Mongol conquerors decided to place their northern gate about here. Seven centuries later, Herzog & de Meuron landed the Olympic stadium bid with its 'Bird's Nest', partly thanks to input from Beijing art luminary Ai Weiwei, who later cursed the creation in a tirade against the regime. The 80,000-seat arena swallowed up some half a billion dollars in its construction, but no one was counting the cost when the structure wowed the world. Since then, however, there have been questions about what to do with it – tourism revenue struggles to come close to the $22m annual operating bill. So now, as long as it pays, anything goes – from a Jackie Chan concert to the Italian football Super Cup and a winter sports park with ski slopes.
Olympic Green, T 8437 3008

HOTELS

WHERE TO STAY AND WHICH ROOMS TO BOOK

The first global five-star hotel to open in Beijing was The Great Wall Sheraton (10 Dongsanhuan Beilu, T 6590 5566), in 1984. Its mirrored glass may seem unsophisticated today, but it symbolises the start of an architectural overhaul. Now, after the glut of hotels developed for the Olympics, most of the luxury chains are here, many located on Jianguomen/Chang'an, the artery that barrels from the CBD to Tiananmen Square, although such inhuman scale makes the surroundings impersonal. The old guard – Raffles (33 Dongchang'an Jie, T 6526 3388) and Shangri-La's China World (1 Jianguomenwai Dajie, T 6505 2266) – stand alongside modern options like the Park Hyatt (2 Jianguomenwai Dajie, T 8567 1234) and W (2 Jianguomennan Dajie, T 6515 8855), and the brands keep coming, with the Four Seasons (48 Liangmaqiao Lu, T 5695 8888), Mandarin Oriental (see p011) and Waldorf Astoria (see p028).

Fortunately, there has also been a flowering of boutique hotels. The trend began in 2006 with Hotel Kapok (16 Donghuamen Dajie, T 6525 9988) and the scene has been strengthened by additions such as Grace (see p026), The Emperor (opposite) and, a real gem hidden in the alleyways, The Orchid (65 Baochao Hutong, T 8404 4818). And then, of course, there's The Opposite House (see p030), which – all hyperbole aside – raised the bar to an entirely new level on opening in 2008, and remains the one hoteliers want to beat. *For full addresses and room rates, see Resources.*

The Emperor Qianmen

This local brand's second launch is as accomplished as its first, The Emperor Forbidden City (T 6526 5566), known for its rooftop bar and jacuzzi. The Emperor Qianmen, a short stroll from Tiananmen Square, goes one step further with the city's first open-air rooftop pool and bar, which provide views of Zhengyangmen, an imperial-era gate. It's an apt touch given that the hotel occupies the site of an old public bath (its marble facade still stands nearby), and designer Dan Euser's indoor 'rainfall' installations (above) continue the theme. The 65 contemporary rooms come in five monochrome designs – the Miracle Suite (overleaf) has black slate walls, dark polished wood floors and an intricate LED chandelier dangling down above the bed. *87 Xianyukou Jie, T 6701 7790, www.theemperor.com.cn*

The Temple Hotel

In 2007, Juan van Wassenhove, Lin Fan and Li Chow took up a five-year challenge to convert an old Qing dynasty temple and its surrounding buildings, including a Mao-era factory. The resulting Temple Hotel is an exemplar of conservation, carried out at a time when developers have been quick to tear down the past. Restored using original tiles and wood (reception area, opposite), it won a UNESCO award. The eight delightful rooms (Twilight, above) marry historical references with modern design elements, including the bamboo desks by Sandeep Sangaru, statement pieces by Shang Xia (see p089) and lighting by Ingo Maurer. The compound is also a draw for its fine-dining restaurant (see p046) and James Turrell's only permanent light installation in China. *23 Shatan Beijie, T 8401 5680, www.thetemplehotel.com*

Hotel Côté Cour

Can Beijing ever have too many courtyard
hotels? If they are all as charming as the
Côté Cour, then no, especially as the old
hutong where these boutique properties
are found are in grave danger of being lost
forever. There are just 14 rooms, including
the Superior Suite (opposite), which lead
off a tranquil courtyard with a koi pond
(above); your stay here will be a peaceful
one. The interiors are all about classical
Chinese decadence – ancient brick floors,
sumptuous silks and Tibetan rugs – while
the main front gate embraces the ancient
traditions of this 500-year-old site with
two guardian lion statues and a red screen
wall believed to protect the building from
evil spirits. The Côté Cour can be somewhat
tricky to find, but it's well worth the effort
for a taste of a China being swallowed up
by an unstoppable drive for modernisation.
70 Yanyue Hutong, T 6523 9598,
www.hotelcotecourbj.com

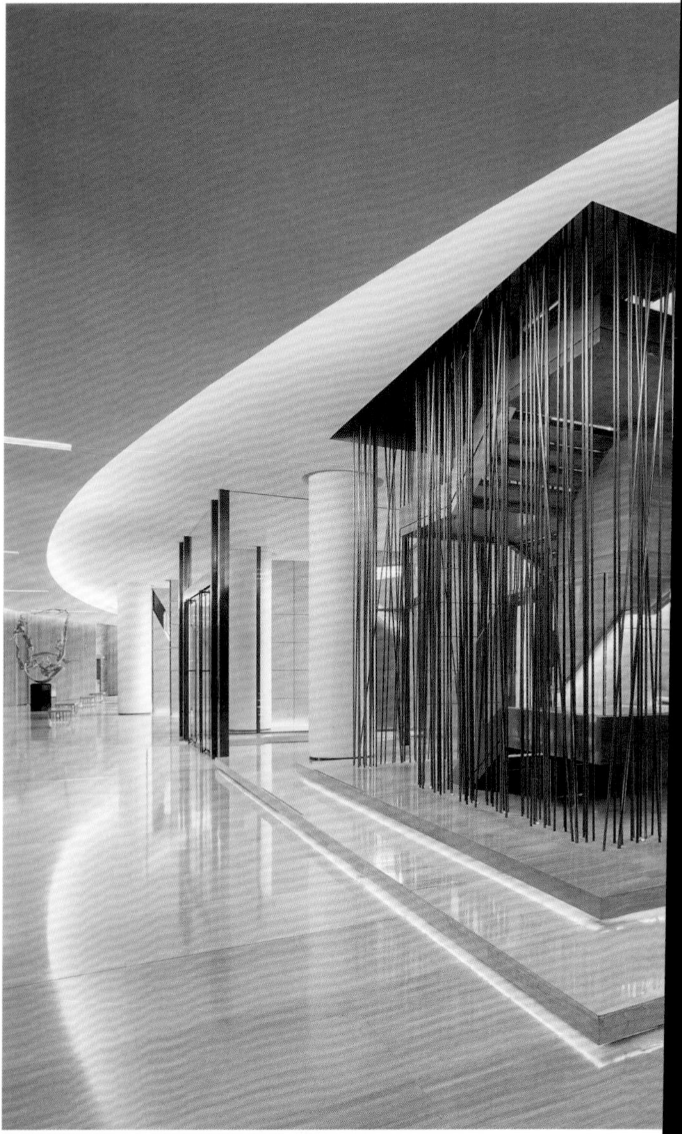

EAST

Business hotels usually equate commerce with conservatism. Not so at EAST, where the concerns of the executive traveller are met with the expected efficiency, but also a sense of style and fun, thanks to Neri & Hu's refreshing design of the public areas (left). And so the common-or-garden meeting spaces, the free and fast wi-fi, and the pool and fitness area are enhanced by one of the city's best hotel bars, with an aesthetic inspired by the industrial spaces of the nearby 798 Art District (see p072), and a communal area that mixes workstations and a reading room with a lounge and café – not to mention chairs by Ronan and Erwan Bouroullec. The 369 rooms, designed by Benoy, feature oak, panoramic windows and headboard art by Zhang Shulan. Usefully, EAST is located 20 minutes from both airport and downtown.
22 Jiuxianqiao Lu, T 8426 0888, www.east-beijing.com

Grace

Carved out of an old crystal factory deep in the 798/751 area (see p072), Grace offers accommodation worthy of the artistic and architectural heritage of its surroundings. There is a hint of Beijing-meets-Bauhaus about the facade, while the lovely interior by Shauna Liu, who made her name at Côté Cour (see p022), manages to merge Ming dynasty inspiration and old-world Asia with art deco. A changing rota of modern Chinese art includes photography by Chi Peng in the spacious Grace Suite (above), the pick of the 30 rooms. The restaurant, named Yi House in honour of the hotel's original name, serves Mediterranean and Asian cuisine, and has a focus on seafood. Expect to hang out with a creative crowd here during design and fashion weeks. *2 Jiuxianqiao Lu, T 6436 1818, www.gracehotels.com*

Aman at Summer Palace

Set next to the east gate of the Summer Palace (T 6288 1144), one of the city's most beautiful sites, Aman's impressive resort borrows inspiration from its neighbour. The suites, such as the Imperial (above), surround an internal courtyard, with the dwellings here sumptuously updated from the days when they were occupied by guests of the Empress Dowager Cixi in the late 19th century. Designed by Jaya Ibrahim with Jean-Michel Gathy, the hotel has a library and several elegant courtyard restaurants; we like the Japanese eaterie Naoki. There's also a private entrance to the Palace. A word of warning: while Aman might well boast a resident calligrapher, it is not the most convenient option if you need to travel across the city to the CBD. *1 Gongmenqian Jie, T 5987 9999, www.amanresorts.com*

Waldorf Astoria

The brand arrived in Beijing in 2014, the year the iconic Waldorf Astoria New York was bought by China's Anbang Insurance Group for $1.95bn – a sign of how times have changed. You can't miss the hotel's striking bronze facade, designed by AS+GG and RTKL, just off the main shopping drag of Wangfujing. Yabu Pushelberg's interior includes 171 rooms (Terrace Suite, above) and incorporates Chinese-inspired design elements such as silk-panelled walls; the impressive contemporary art includes work by Ling Jian, Luo Xiaodong and Shao Fan. Connected via underground passage are two Hutong Villas (opposite); styled as traditional *siheyuan* (courtyard houses). One boasts a pool and a mini-cinema and the other is split into four separate studios.
5-15 Jinyu Hutong, T 8520 8989, www.waldorfastoria.com

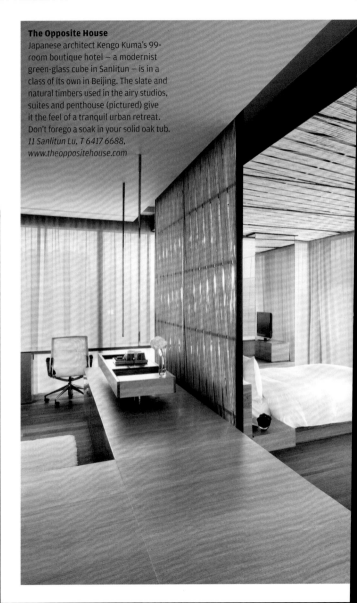

The Opposite House
Japanese architect Kengo Kuma's 99-room boutique hotel – a modernist green-glass cube in Sanlitun – is in a class of its own in Beijing. The slate and natural timbers used in the airy studios, suites and penthouse (pictured) give it the feel of a tranquil urban retreat. Don't forego a soak in your solid oak tub.
11 Sanlitun Lu, T 6417 6688,
www.theoppositehouse.com

24 HOURS

SEE THE BEST OF THE CITY IN JUST ONE DAY

Beijing is a historic capital where the sites are all too often drably explained. Thankfully, the splendour of its imperial-era attractions more than speaks for itself. The Temple of Heaven (opposite) is the least tourist-clogged introduction to what remains from the days of emperors and dynasties. Those willing to brave the crowds may prefer to explore the Forbidden City (see p012); climb the hill in Jingshan Park, just to the north, for one of the best views in town. Mao's mausoleum (overleaf) on the opposite side of the palace is a constant reminder of the man who changed China like no other.

Beijing's intellectual and art scenes, meanwhile, are crucial in its quest for an identity. Long before the Olympics, it was the avant-garde that breathed credibility back into this hugely creative city. Aficionados should find the time to travel out to Caochangdi – Ai Weiwei's art enclave on the north-eastern outskirts – as well as the influential UCCA gallery in the 798 Art District (see p072).

This isn't much of a walking city, but there are parts you can happily cover on foot. The hutong south of Tiananmen Square are worth exploring, thanks to redevelopment driven by an influx of like-minded creatives, nowhere more so than at Re-Up (see p036). Nor should you leave Beijing without trying the duck (see p038). End the evening with cocktails at D Lounge (see p039) or Janes & Hooch (see p050), before dancing on the roof at Migas (see p052). *For full addresses, see Resources.*

08.00 Temple of Heaven

Built in the 15th century, at the same time as the Forbidden City (see p012), this was where the Chinese emperors came to make sacrifices and pray for prosperity. The main temple, the Hall of Prayer for Good Harvests (above), with its triple-eaved blue-tiled roof, is particularly striking, and something of an architectural marvel. The 38m-tall wooden building was constructed without the use of a single nail and the walls carry no weight; the load is instead transferred to the 28 columns. It is best experienced first thing in the morning; most of the key sites in the complex open at 8am, although the 273-hectare park can be entered from 6am, when it comes alive with Beijing's older residents singing, exercising and playing cards or mah-jong. *Tiantan Gongyuan, T 6702 8866, www.tiantanpark.com*

10.00 Chairman Mao Memorial Hall

Major architectural projects in China have long been intended to make statements about the nation, and nowhere is this more apparent than the Chairman Mao Memorial Hall. Built in just six months by 700,000 citizens, and opened in 1977, exactly one year after he passed away, Mao Zedong's mausoleum symbolically used materials sourced from all over the country, including rocks from the Kunlun Mountains, sand from the Taiwan Strait and clay from Mao's birthplace of Shaoshan. It was also placed directly on the city's central axis, its north-facing entrance deliberately blocking the old imperial sight line from the Forbidden City. It's open Tuesday to Sunday, 8am to noon. Note that bags and cameras must be deposited at a storage facility before you queue up to see Mao's embalmed remains.
South Tiananmen Square, T 6513 2277

12.00 Re-Up

Championing a nascent and much-needed sustainability movement, this multi-use space encompasses a stylish café, sells upcycled and eco-conscious products and hosts talks on responsible living. It was conceived by Lin Lin (see p062), who, with architect Andy Bryant, converted a 1950s art deco-style factory into a community hub. A lean, minimal interior embraces the ethos by using salvaged hardwood and local materials, and the work by emerging artists hanging on the walls is for sale. The menu features conscientiously sourced ingredients, some grown hyper-locally in the aquaponic roof garden, and comprises a creative fusion of East and West in treats such as the sweet potato and duck rice ball and the hot chocolate with chilli flakes. There's also a top sommelier here.
59 Tieshu Xiejie, T 6248 5863, www.re-up.cn

15.00 Hutong tour

Beijing's ecosystem of alleyways is slowly dying, despite promises of protection. UNESCO estimates that during the last 30 years nearly 90 per cent of the hutong have been demolished. Preservation is often code for prettification – relics are saved but traditional homes are gutted. The Disneyfication of Qianmen has been a commercial breakthrough but a cultural disaster, while Nanluoguxiang is held up as the model of successful regeneration but has become too popular for its own good, and struggles to maintain its charm. Instead, try the quirky Wudaoying hutong, near the Lama Temple, and Fangjia, a few lanes further south. These neighbourhoods are rejuvenating with creative boutiques, bars and cafés. The previously neglected hutong around Dashilar (opposite) are also offering an insight into a brighter future.

20.00 Duck de Chine

There are several Peking duck specialists worth trying, including Da Dong (see p055) and Jing Yaa Tang (T 6410 5230) at The Opposite House, a collaboration with Alan Yau, but only one with a neo-industrial interior, all exposed beams and bare-brick walls. The restaurant is housed in one of the city's more successful redevelopment projects: 1949 – The Hidden City, a small factory complex reimagined by George Wang in 2008. There's a French twist to the menu but the real draw here is the duck, cooked over wood for longer than normal to get rid of excess fat (the preparation time means it must be pre-ordered). Enjoy with the traditional accompaniments of pancakes, spring onions and plum sauce. *1949 – The Hidden City, Courtyard Four, off Gongti Beilu, T 6501 8881, www.elite-concepts.com*

22.00 D Lounge

Beijing bar interiors don't get much better than this, possibly the capital's slickest drinking spot. Top cocktails, relaxed music, well-designed furniture and modern art add atmosphere, but the space itself is the star. The high ceilings, soaring arches and raw brickwork lend an air of factory-meets-fashionista, while the white bar towers above like a bacchanalian temple – more Gaudí than gaudy. Li Bo, who founded D Lounge with Warren Pang (see p050), conceived the design, which was executed by Sky Deng. The crowd here is the most sophisticated of those drawn to this now-buzzing part of town, also home to nightlife favourites such as Taco Bar (T 6501 6026), a buzzing tequila den, and the burger-and-beer basics of The Local (T 6591 9525).
*4 Gongti Beilu, T 6593 7710,
www.dlounge.com.cn*

URBAN LIFE
CAFÉS, RESTAURANTS, BARS AND NIGHTCLUBS

Beijing has a way to go before its nightlife can be compared to that of London or New York. Nevertheless, it does encourage locals and visitors alike to have fun. Most of the action takes place in the east, amid the perennial buzz of Sanlitun and Gongti, or among the hip hutong of Gulou. But it's a mammoth, evolving city, and anything can be found if you know where to look. Indeed, foodies can embark on a culinary voyage across China without leaving the capital due to some fine regional restaurants. Standouts are the Manchurian cuisine at Najia Xiaoguan (10 Yonganli, T 6568 6553), Sichuanese at Chuan Ban (5 Gongyuantoutiao, T 6512 2277) and Yunnanese at Lost Heaven (23 Qianmen Dongdajie, T 8516 2698), or try the dumplings at Din Tai Fung (24 Xinyuanxili Zhongjie, T 6462 4502).

The live music scene provides a glimpse of the counterculture, at venues such as Yu Gong Yi Shan (3-2 Zhangzizhong Lu, T 6404 2711) and Mao Live (111 Gulou Dongdajie, T 6402 5080). Clubbers flock to Mix (Workers' Stadium, T 6530 2889) or the hip Dada (206 Gulou Dongdajie, T 183 1108 0818), while Destination (7 Gongti Xilu, T 6552 8180) is a gay wonderland. For a liquid tour of Beijing, sample the beer at microbreweries Great Leap (12 Xinzhong Jie, T 6416 6887) and Slow Boat (56 Dongsibatiao, T 6538 5537), original cocktails at Mao Mao Chong (see p054) and China's notoriously strong *baijiu* at Capital Spirits (3 Daju Hutong, T 6409 3319). *For full addresses, see Resources.*

Susu

Husband-and-wife team Jonathan Ansfield and Amy Li ran the lakeside Stone Boat Café in Ritan Park for five years before being forced out in 2009. When they found the site for Vietnamese restaurant Susu, they enlisted Kupa Studios to remodel it, and went upmarket. The team kept the courtyard footprint of the 19th-century building, refurbished and exposed its original pillars and beams, extended the bar area, installed full-height windows and added a terrace. The native chefs bring an authenticity to dishes such as *món canh* (sour fish soup, cooked in a clay pot). Ansfield's day job at *The New York Times* means this hutong hideaway draws the foreign press corps, alongside a hip crowd sampling the quality cocktails.
10 Qiangliang Xixiang, T 8400 2699, www.susubeijing.com

Green T House Living
This wonderfully chic suburban retreat
comprises a teahouse, gallery, gardens
and a spa-turned-restaurant with big
communal tables, set by a tea-scented
pool. Much of the modernist furniture is
designed by artist-musician owner JinR.
The fine contemporary Chinese cuisine
is theatrically and beautifully presented.
*318 Cuige Zhuang Xiang, Hege Zhuang
Cun, T 6434 2519*

Capital M

The 1999 launch of Shanghai's M on the Bund by Melbourne restaurateur Michelle Garnaut kickstarted the waterfront revival. Consequently, few Beijing restaurants have been as keenly anticipated as Capital M, seven years in the making, which opened in 2009. The food is mod Med with a few Middle Eastern and North African dishes, and service is superb, but most impressive is the interior by Debra Little and Roger Hackworth, with monochrome art deco floor tiles, and a 50m hand-painted mural by Australian Michael Cartwright. Metres from the old gate near Tiananmen Square, it's also perfect for rooftop sundowners. The events space hosts regular talks on architecture or contemporary art, and a hugely successful annual literary festival. *3rd floor, 2 Qianmen Dajie, T 6702 2727, www.m-restaurant-group.com/capitalm*

Brian McKenna at The Courtyard

American lawyer Handel Lee went on to oversee the development of Three on the Bund in Shanghai and Beijing's Legation Quarter after cementing his reputation at The Courtyard. A fine-dining East-West-fusion restaurant and art gallery in a renovated Qing dynasty building, it was a real first for the capital in 1997. But in a fast-moving city, it struggled to stay relevant. Enter Brian McKenna in 2013, who had previously enthralled locals with his molecular cuisine at the Shangri-La. Here, he has brought that innovation and experimentation to an equally impressive space, next to the Forbidden City's East Gate. The room itself was sleekly refreshed by GRAFT; request a table with a view of the imperial palace's moat and walls. *95 Donghuamen Dajie, T 6526 8883, www.bmktc.com*

TRB

When Ignace Lecleir left Michelin-starred Daniel's in New York to help set up Boulud's outpost in Beijing in 2008, he introduced unparalleled service to a city known for its surliness. He launched his own place, TRB, within the grounds of an abandoned 600-year-old temple in 2011. It remains a destination thanks to Lecleir's effortless touch, its classic European-inspired cuisine and gracefully judged interiors by Hassell that exalt the beauty of the architecture with splashes of colour and light. Note the original stone archway and timber as you enter through the bar and cross to the dining area via a walkway. This part of the complex – also home to a lovely hotel (see p020) – was a TV factory inserted into the old temple by workers under Mao. *23 Shatan Beijie, T 8400 2232, www.trb-cn.com*

Okra
Architect Phil Dunn and designer Sean
Dix converted a meat-slicing factory
into a 38-seat sushi and sake bar for US
chef Max Levy. Subtle touches include
Erwin Hauer-style okra-pattern panels.
There's a genuine focus on provenance,
and the world-class sushi has Chinese
twists, like the red tofu (not miso) soup.
*1949 – The Hidden City, Courtyard Four,
off Gongti Beilu, T 6593 5087*

Janes & Hooch

Sophisticated but unpretentious, Janes & Hooch has developed a loyal following within Beijing's mutating cocktail circuit. Opened in 2012 – at a time when the city was totally seduced by speakeasy-inspired saloons – its owners, Warren Pang and Milan Sekulic, brought a refreshing sense of style and service to the scene. Modern industrial elements combine with an old-school aesthetic that harks back to the golden era of cocktails, and drinks are crafted by dapper, sharp-talking staff. It's not all about the nostalgia though, since the negronis here are often served up to a hip-hop soundtrack, and a rotating menu keeps things fresh. We ordered the Blood & Spice: Spice Tree scotch, apricot brandy, red vermouth and blood orange. *Courtyard Four, Gongti Beilu, T 6503 2757, www.janeshooch.com*

Dali Courtyard

Set in a hutong, Dali serves cuisine from the south-west province of Yunnan that borders Vietnam, Laos and Burma, which is far removed from the usual Cantonese and north Chinese fare. The kitchen sends out dishes based on what is available on the day, and the RMB150 set menu means you don't need to read the lingo to sample these regional delicacies. Highlights have included delicately spiced mushrooms, mint-infused tofu, grilled tilapia with lemongrass, and ginseng, goji berry and bamboo soup. Book an alfresco table in summer or retreat to the warmth of the rustic rooms (above) in winter. Such has been the success of this local gem that a second courtyard space, Dali Village (T 6455 3956), has opened 300m away. *67 Xiaojingchang Hutong, off Gulou Dongdajie, T 8404 1430*

Migas
On summer evenings there's no bigger
party than on Migas' funky roof, often
soundtracked by big-name DJs. The
restaurant (pictured) is a destination
too thanks to creative Basque chef Aitor
Olabegoya, and an interior by Pichiglas
that includes an egg chandelier, graphic
art by Eltono and graffiti by Sixeart.
*6th floor, Nali Patio, 81 Sanlitun Beilu,
T 5208 6061, www.migasbj.com*

Q Bar

Beijing can be bizarre sometimes – take Q, one of the city's best cocktail bars, installed above one of its ugliest hotels. First-timers often arrive at the dull Eastern Inn and assume they're in the wrong place, but a cool lounge awaits on the sixth floor. The terrace, co-designed by owner Echo Sun, is dotted with sheltered alcoves lined with woven tatami panels, and is particularly popular in summer. Q's opening in 2006 sowed the seeds for a flourishing cocktail culture. Also highly recommended are George's (T 6553 6299), run by one of Q's original partners; Apothecary (T 5208 6040), which began a trend for homemade bitters and syrups; and the chilled Mao Mao Chong (T 6405 5718), which brought innovative mixology to the old alleys.
Eastern Inn, Sanlitun Nanlu/Gongti Nanlu, T 6595 9239, www.qbarbeijing.com

Da Dong

Celebrity chef culture is yet to grip the Middle Kingdom, but one name everyone knows is Da Dong, aka Dong Zhenxiang, whose empire of eponymous restaurants (see p082) serves some of the best *kaoya* (Peking duck) in town. Dong has more than 30 years of experience and has developed a method of cooking the bird that delivers lean, crispy skin but juicy meat. He also applies molecular gastronomy in dishes such as double-boiled bird's nest with rose jelly. Few homegrown chefs are so intent on pushing the boundaries of their national cuisine. Set within a complex of Ming-era granaries, Dong's Nanxincang outpost has an interior designed by the man himself, inspired by Chinese ceramics. More often than not, it's the most buzzing of them all. *1st and 2nd floors, Nanxincang Guoji Dasha, 22 Dongsishitiao, T 5169 0329*

Transit
Given its location in a mall, Transit has
a lovely moody interior, with touches of
chinoiserie, created by co-owner Kevin
Zhao, who designed the furniture and
lights. His sister Grace produces high-end
Sichuanese cuisine with a modern twist,
from typically hot, numbing dishes to
milder ones, using little oil and no MSG.
N4-36, 3rd floor, Taikoo Li North,
Sanlitun Lu, T6417 9090

Moka Bro's

This Sanlitun haunt is hands-down Beijing's coolest café. It's to be expected given that, prior to opening here in 2013, owners Alex Molina and Daniel Urdaneta had proved themselves with the casual, modern dining at Mosto (T 5208 6030), followed by Modo (T 6415 7207), a contemporary deli. Both remain firm local favourites, and have won Venezuelan chef Urdaneta and Colombian manager Molina a loyal following. Moka's success has been to make healthy eating cool, and to do so in stylish surroundings. China's increasingly fashion-conscious millennials descend here for their dose of quinoa and kale, taking inspiration from the feel-good slogans plastered across the white tiles. Another cute touch by design company Coromoto is the skeletal ceiling lights, created by stripping traditional Chinese lanterns of their silk.

Ground floor, Nali Patio, 81 Sanlitun Beilu, T 5208 6079, www.mokabros.com

Ichikura

A big trend in Beijing's nightlife scene has been the rise and rise of the whisky bar. The finest example is Ichikura, which, as with many of the city's best hangouts, is hard to find. In this instance, you'll need to clamber the rickety stairs to the right of the Chaoyang Theatre – think of it as a homage to the acrobats that perform there. Once inside, you will find a sleek space with a wonderfully calm ambience and more than 400 whiskies on offer, but just 12 seats, allowing Japanese manager Koji Kuroki to provide some of the finest service that you'll find this side of Tokyo. Watching him pour a dram of Yamazaki over a beautifully hand-carved sphere of ice is quite simply a delight. For an equally charming experience in the hutong, seek out courtyard bar Amilal (T 8404 1416). *36 Dongsanhuan Beilu, T 6507 1107*

Noodle Bar

Chinese food is still too often regarded as convenient takeaway. But fast doesn't have to mean forlorn, and a noodle fix needn't equate to getting down and dirty, at least not when smart venues such as this prove that simple staples can be eaten with a certain degree of style. Set behind a modest door in the appropriately named Hidden City – a former Sanlitun factory complex turned entertainment

destination (see p038) – the timber-clad room has just 12 seats and three counters, set around an open kitchen, adding to the intimacy. The menu is straightforward too, with a focus on beef soup and a selection of basic sides. Chefs prepare your order in front of you, pulling the noodles by hand, adding a little theatre to the proceedings.
1949 – The Hidden City, Courtyard Four, off Gongti Beilu, T 6501 1949

INSIDER'S GUIDE
LIN LIN, CREATIVE DIRECTOR, JELLYMON

The Chinese have their own term, *haigui* (sea turtle), for the reverse brain drain phenomenon – those who have lived abroad but return to pursue careers. Lin Lin studied in Singapore and London, where she co-founded the creative agency Jellymon, which she now runs from Beijing. 'It's uncompromising but there's something majestic about the city,' she says. 'It's changed so much, and is still rushing forward.' In response, in 2014, Lin Lin founded the community hub Re-Up (see p036), dedicated to the rejuvenation of the hutong.

'The best breakfast is always on the street,' she says. Her pick is the *doufunao* (bean curd) and *youtiao* (fried dough sticks) 'down the alley two west of Sanlitun Lu, opposite the hospital'. She also recommends the home cooking and vegetable hotpot at Tai Shu Xi (south of east gate, Tuanjiehu Park, T 8598 4766), and Si Ji Min Fu (8 Langfang Ertiao, T 6301 8796), where it's 'cheap, loud and fun, with the best *zhajiangmian* (noodles and minced pork) in the city'.

Lin Lin often has coffee in Soloist (39 Yangmeizhu Xiejie, T 5711 1717), for its vintage interiors, or Café Zarah (42 Gulou Dongdajie, T 8403 9807), located in a courtyard house with an industrial vibe. Her favourite bars include Modernista (44 Baochao Hutong, T 136 9142 5744), Janes & Hooch (see p050) and Mokihi (3rd floor, C12 Haoyun Jie, T 5867 0244): 'A quirky place with quality cocktails.' But Migas (see p052) has 'the best terrace and the best parties'. *For full addresses, see Resources.*

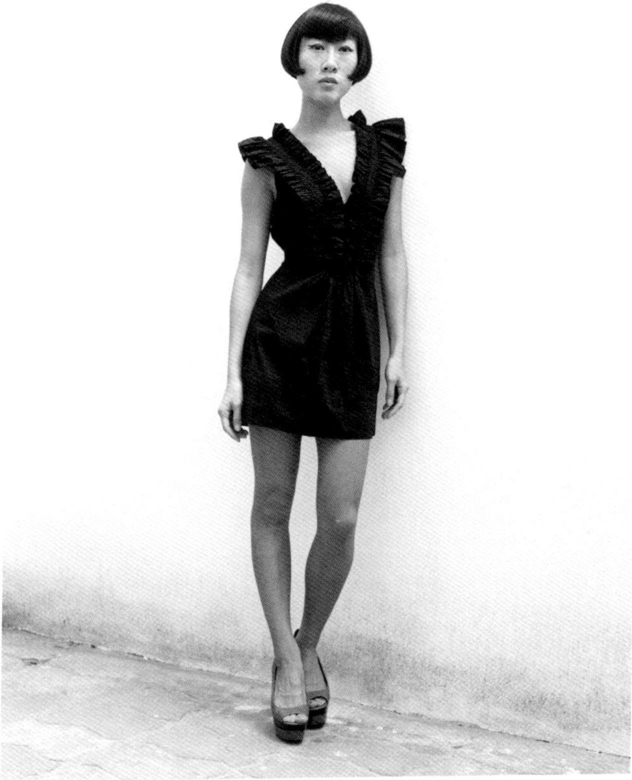

ART AND DESIGN

GALLERIES, STUDIOS AND PUBLIC SPACES

The story of Beijing's art scene is the story of China. Millennia of civilisation has resulted in a wealth of historical treasures, from pottery to calligraphy and ink-and-wash paintings – NAMOC (see p078) gives a fine overview. But with the onset of communism in 1949, creative pursuits came under attack, no more so than during the Cultural Revolution (1966-76) under Mao, when all aesthetic activity was extinguished, and cultural artefacts destroyed.

It wasn't just business that bounced back when Deng Xiaoping reopened the country in the 1980s – a shackled art world also made up for lost time. A movement sprang into being as experimental protagonists formed outlying 'villages' (see p076). As the ideas flowed, so did the money; the extraordinary boom was such that in 2011 China overtook the US as the world's biggest art market, and the likes of Zeng Fanzhi (see p068) and Zhang Xiaogang became household names. These days, cutting-edge art is found across the city, from top hotels to dedicated areas such as the 798 Art District (see p072), Pingguo (see p074) and Caochangdi (see p076).

Chinese design has struggled to keep pace – with the exception of the venerable CAFA institute (overleaf). However, the grassroots outlook is now showing far more promise, as studios, ateliers and workshops open in the hutong. Beijing Design Week, which began in 2011 and is growing in stature, is helping drive this evolution. *For full addresses, see Resources.*

Shao Fan

Painter, sculptor and designer Shao Fan was one of the first people in China to blur the lines between these mediums. Born to a family of creatives and intellectuals, he studied at Beijing Arts and Crafts College, and made his breakthrough in the mid-1990s with the 'Chairs' series, in which he reconstructed traditional furniture using contemporary materials and aesthetics as an expression of the changes China was undergoing at that time. When the V&A Museum in London acquired a number of these pieces, he became the first modern-day Chinese artist to be exhibited there. To see Shao Fan's work in Beijing, make a pilgrimage to Galerie Urs Meile (T 6433 3393) in Caochangdi Village (see p077), which has his 'Steel Chair' (above) in its portfolio, as well as a selection of oils, inks, prints and sculptures.

CAFA Art Museum
The Central Academy of Fine Arts (CAFA)
is the most prestigious in China. Only 10
per cent of applicants are accepted into
this state-run institution, which covers a
range of disciplines from fine art to urban
design and Chinese painting – alumni
include Zhang Huan, Sui Jianguo and Xu
Bing. In 2008, a six-floor museum opened
within its Wangjing campus, designed
by Japanese architect Arata Isozaki, who
wrapped its curves in traditional native
slate and kept the interior whitewashed
and flooded with daylight. Exhibitions
rotate between selections from CAFA's own
collection of ancient and modern Chinese
masters, and – of great interest to the
increasing numbers of those clamouring
to discover The Next Big Thing – work by
the best of its recent graduates.
8 Huajiadi Nanjie, T 6477 1575,
museum.cafa.com.cn

Yuan Space

When Zeng Fanzhi's *The Last Supper* sold for $23.3m in 2013, it set a record for an Asian contemporary work, and made him China's highest-selling artist. Now in his fifties, Zeng is bankrolling Yuan Space and has ambitious plans for it to become the country's leading museum for international art. It will be housed in a distinctive five-storey building with a typically geometric silhouette by Tadao Ando, located in the Embassy District and set to open in 2017. Before that, make an appointment to visit this transitional space, which acts as a training ground for staff, and has hosted exhibitions featuring Andrew Wyeth and Yu Youhan. The permanent collection already includes work by important 20th-century Western artists such as Giorgio Morandi. *20th floor, Tower B, Jiaming Center, 27 Dongsanhuan Beilu, T 5775 5070*

400ml

One of the capital's most acclaimed graffiti crews is ABS, formed back in 2007 by four artists who have since won a number of prestigious global competitions and toured Europe on cultural exchange programmes. ABS opened 400ml, China's first 'graffiti outlet', in 2012, and it quickly became the unofficial headquarters of a focused group of creatives influencing the local scene. Budding street artists come here to pick up paint, participate in workshops and collaborate on ideas; as well as aerosols, it also sells artwork and graffiti-inspired clothing. Nearby, check out the concrete wall along Jingmi Lu (overleaf) that acts as Beijing's hall of fame. Further west, the streets around Gulou Dongdajie are also now filling up with ABS-inspired activity. *798 Art District, 4 Jiuxianqiao Lu, T 5978 4865*

Graffiti wall, Jingmi Lu

798 Art District

It was in Dashanzi that Beijing's radical artists first stumbled on a post-industrial 'promised land', the Maoist slogans on the walls providing a powerful if gimmicky context. The area was soon dubbed 798, after the Bauhaus-style factory at its core. The influential UCCA (T 5780 0200), which opened in 2007, became a big player, and 798 is now a hub of art spaces and cafés. Notable galleries include US transplant Pace (T 5978 9781), which focuses on solo exhibitions by Chinese artists who have established a global reputation, such as Yin Xiuzhen (*Nowhere to Land*, opposite). For something more under the radar, arrange a visit to the Gao Brothers' studio (T 8459 9577; appointment only). Their politically charged creations (*Miss Mao*, above) have resulted in past shows being shut down.
Jiuxianqiao Lu, Dashanzi, www.798art.org

Today Art Museum
Financed by the real-estate mogul Zhang
Baoquan, this red-brick former brewery
and boiler house, fronted by Yue Minjun's
'laughing' statues, was converted into
a museum by Wang Hui in 2002. It has
since morphed into two other buildings
and is an anchor for the community in
the Pingguo complex, one of the few art
hubs that's located close to the CBD.
32 Baiziwan Lu, T 5876 0600

Three Shadows Photography Art Centre
Those in search of Beijing's avant-garde in the early 1990s would have found it in the so-called 'East Village', where a group of cutting-edge performance artists lived and worked together on the city fringes. This key period in Chinese art history was documented via the lens of Rong Rong, one of the photographers among their number. Today, the most revered artistic centre and its main players are found in Caochangdi Village, which is similarly on the outskirts, with Ai Weiwei at its heart and Rong Rong's influence still keenly felt through his own gallery, Three Shadows, which he runs with his Japanese wife Inri. The 4,600 sq m complex, which opened in 2007, is the first space in China to be solely dedicated to photography and video art.
155a Caochangdi, T 6432 2663,
www.threeshadows.cn

NAMOC

Established by Mao Zedong in 1958, the National Art Museum of China (NAMOC) is funded by the Ministry of Culture. Its regularly changing exhibitions draw on an extensive collection that stretches across both history and style: ancient Chinese art shares wall space with contemporary objects from the West. The museum suffers somewhat from a lack of a permanent display to provide some context but this should be rectified by 2016, when its new home will be unveiled near the National Stadium (see p014) in the Olympic Park. Designed by Jean Nouvel, the forthcoming building features a perforated facade that encloses a six-storey atrium and an indoor garden. The gallery will be seven times larger than the current incarnation and is expected to attract 12m visitors a year. *1 Wusi Dajie, T 6400 1476, www.namoc.org*

Pékin Fine Arts

This agenda-setting gallery is housed in a purpose-built space designed by Ai Weiwei. Consisting of three 200 sq m exhibition rooms as well as a sculpture garden, it is pleasingly simple – the grey brick, which imitates hutong architecture, is mixed with industrial touches such as strip lighting. Established back in 2005, Pékin's success is down to the involvement of Bostonian Meg Maggio, who moved to China in 1986.

Her impressive reputation, gained in the 1990s when she ran one of Beijing's first private galleries, has helped her build a high degree of trust among artists (work by Yan Lei from the 'Post-Photography' exhibition, above) and collectors alike. Pékin sells more pieces to major global museums than any of its rivals in China.
241 Caochangdi, T 5127 3220,
www.pekinfinearts.com

ARCHITOUR

A GUIDE TO BEIJING'S ICONIC BUILDINGS

China's schizophrenic past is reflected in its architecture. Beijing has been a testing ground in the search for a vernacular, some say to its misfortune. A drive for modernism came in 1959 with the 10th birthday of the People's Republic heralded by '10 great buildings' constructed in 10 months, including the Great Hall of the People (west of Tiananmen Square, T 6309 6935), National Museum of China (east of Tiananmen Square, T 6511 6400) and Beijing Railway Station (Beijing Huochezhan). Thirty years of skeletal tenements followed, broken only by Mao's mausoleum (see p034).

In the late 1980s, the MO became a 'socialist market economy with Chinese characteristics'. Postmodern designs with imperial roofs and ornamental pagodas appeared. The city started looking up, as towers like Capital Mansion (6 Xinyuan Nanlu) pierced the horizontal skyline. The Olympics saw Beijing embrace the future with ambitious projects not only limited to sports stadia, including the NCPA (see p084). The zeal continues with Zaha Hadid's office/ retail hub Galaxy Soho (7a Xiaopaifang Hutong), shortlisted for RIBA's Lubetkin Prize, and the inventive Parkview Green (overleaf). The CBD is continually climbing, and will be triumphantly crowned in 2018 by Zhongguo Zun (Guanghua Lu), designed by TFP Farrells and KPF; set to top half a kilometre, it embodies the self-confidence evident as soon as you arrive in Foster + Partners' Terminal 3. *For full addresses, see Resources.*

Linked Hybrid

While everyone was obsessing over the National Stadium (see p014), Steven Holl Architects was quietly getting on with the other cutting-edge development of the Olympic construction boom. Completed in 2009, Linked Hybrid is an eight-tower mixed-use complex that has transformed a corner of the city (where the Second Ring Road meets the Airport Expressway) into a dynamic space. The high-rises are linked on their upper floors by a series of bridges, containing galleries, eateries and even a pool, that hover above a large pond. It is one of Beijing's first green residential projects, drawing on a geothermal water source to supply the heating and cooling systems. Visit the arthouse film centre Broadway Cinematheque (T 8438 8258) to experience this 'open city within a city'.
Grand Moma, 1 Xiangheyuan Lu

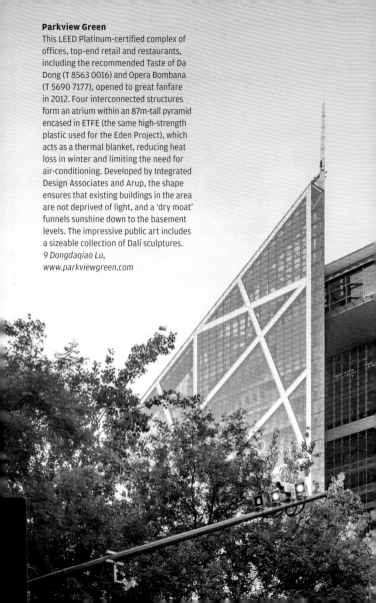

Parkview Green

This LEED Platinum-certified complex of offices, top-end retail and restaurants, including the recommended Taste of Da Dong (T 8563 0016) and Opera Bombana (T 5690 7177), opened to great fanfare in 2012. Four interconnected structures form an atrium within an 87m-tall pyramid encased in ETFE (the same high-strength plastic used for the Eden Project), which acts as a thermal blanket, reducing heat loss in winter and limiting the need for air-conditioning. Developed by Integrated Design Associates and Arup, the shape ensures that existing buildings in the area are not deprived of light, and a 'dry moat' funnels sunshine down to the basement levels. The impressive public art includes a sizeable collection of Dalí sculptures.
9 Dongdaqiao Lu,
www.parkviewgreen.com

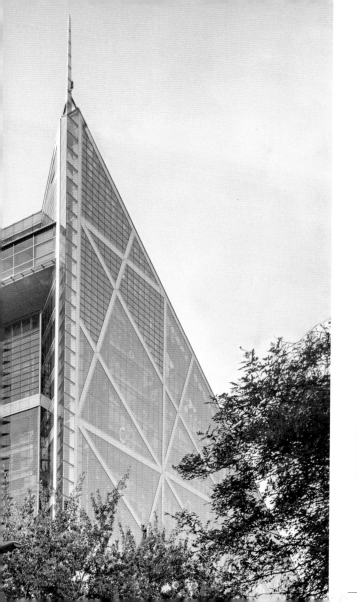

NCPA

When French architect Paul Andreu won the 1998-99 competition to fill the 'big pit' beside the Great Hall of the People (see p080), critics were quick to lampoon his 'floating' bubble of titanium (broken by a swooping glass section reminiscent of a stage curtain) as everything from a duck egg to a dung pile. But defenders saw an iota of Chinese thinking in its circle-in-square geometry. The final verdict on the 2007 National Centre for the Performing Arts (NCPA), aka The Egg, is now in, and it's safe to say that Andreu has indeed created an iconic building that's become part of the fabric of the city and a cultural engine to boot. The venue regularly hosts world-class classical music, allowing visitors to move from Mao to Mozart in moments.
2 Xichang'an Jie, T 6655 0000, www.chncpa.org

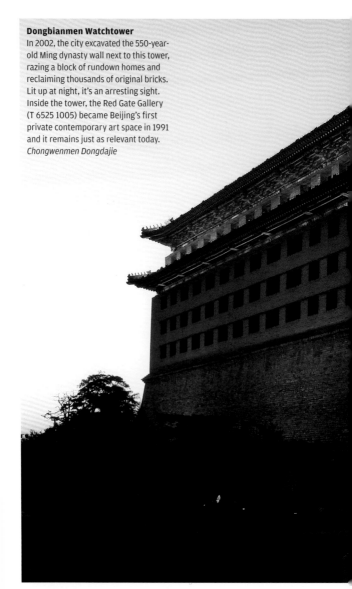

Dongbianmen Watchtower
In 2002, the city excavated the 550-year-old Ming dynasty wall next to this tower, razing a block of rundown homes and reclaiming thousands of original bricks. Lit up at night, it's an arresting sight. Inside the tower, the Red Gate Gallery (T 6525 1005) became Beijing's first private contemporary art space in 1991 and it remains just as relevant today. *Chongwenmen Dongdajie*

SHOPS

THE BEST RETAIL THERAPY AND WHAT TO BUY

It should come as no surprise that, for some, the major attractions of 'the world's factory' are the huge markets selling reproduction goods and kitsch memorabilia. In a clean-up effort, that infamous bazaar of ersatz brand names, Silk Street (8 Xiushui Dongjie, T 5169 9003), was moved indoors in 2005. 'Cheaper, cheaper' China also still lives on at Hongqiao market (46 Tiantan Donglu, T 6713 3354), where you can buy dyed freshwater pearls. A short taxi ride away is the fun Panjiayuan fleamarket (Panjiayuanqiao, T 6775 2405). The 'antiques' sold here are rarely so, but charming curios abound. Continuing the theme in Sanlitun is the Yashow clothing market (58 Gongti Beilu, T 6415 1726); note that haggling is de rigueur.

The rise of the mall seems unstoppable. Find big-name brands at Shin Kong Place (87 Jianguo Lu, T 6530 5888), Seasons Place (2 Jinchengfang Jie, T 6622 0483) and Joy City (131 Xidan Beidajie, T 5833 0000), and still more top flagships in Parkview Green (see p082), Galeries Lafayette (see p090) and Taikoo Li (see p094).

Head to Nali Patio (81 Sanlitun Lu) for independent boutiques, though your best bet for unearthing unique items is to scour Gulou Dongdajie and Nanluoguxiang. Well worth seeking out are Dong Liang (Unit 102, Building 2, Central Park, 6 Chaoyangmenwai Dajie, T 8404 7648) and the hip Triple-Major (81 Baochao Hutong, T 8402 0763), for fashion and design by up-and-coming domestic talent. *For full addresses, see Resources.*

Shang Xia

China has surpassed Japan as the world's largest luxury market due to a seemingly insatiable desire for the West's high-end labels, but the launch of Shang Xia in 2008 signalled the emergence of homegrown players on the global stage. Founded by Jiang Qiong Er, and now backed by Hermès, it is one of the first premium brands in China to marry contemporary design with time-honoured techniques – the furniture, porcelain, jewellery and clothing are all made by artisans reviving ancient skills. Kengo Kuma's interiors beautifully capture the blend of past and future in this 2012 Beijing store. The old neighbourhoods are evoked in the aluminium latticework, and bricks made from compressed tea leaves provide a nod to age-old craftsmanship.
B1 China World Mall, 1 Jianguomenwai Dajie, T 6505 7358, www.shang-xia.com

Christopher Bu

Hugely popular actress Fan Bingbing is also
a hit on the red carpet, no more so than
at Cannes in 2011 and 2012, thanks to the
handiwork of Christopher Bu. Such was
the success of this spotlight – the 2011
'crane dress' auctioned for RMB1m – that
Bu launched two stores in Beijing in 2013.
The first (above) is off Nanluoguxiang, and
functions as both studio and showroom.
Traditional-style roofing references the

hutong location but the interior follows
an atelier-inspired vibe with plenty of
wood and mirrors. The designer's couture
line mixes Western draping and silhouettes
with heavy Chinese hand-embroidery; his
ready-to-wear range is chic, with a touch
of vintage. The second shop has pride of
place in Galeries Lafayette (T 5962 9888).
25 Ju'er Hutong, T 5283 4540,
www.christopherbu.com

Fei Space

Artist and ceramicist Lin Jing's work has sold at 10 Corso Como in Milan and been exhibited at the V&A in London. In Beijing, she transformed her home in the 798 Art District (see p072) into a fashion boutique to create one of the most original shops in town, thanks to bespoke installations such as chandeliers made from rope dog leads (above) and a wrought-iron teepee. This is where locals flock to for international labels that are otherwise hard to find on the mainland, including Alexander Wang, Rebecca Minkoff and Jonathan Saunders. Fei Space also sells rugs from Iran, India and Afghanistan, and, of course, Lin Jing's own tableware – limited runs of vases, cups and plates that take China's venerable ceramic tradition in a modern direction.
B-01, 798 Art District, 2 Jiuxianqiao Lu, T 5978 9580

Spin Ceramics
Produced by master ceramicists from
Hong Kong and Jingdezhen, China's
legendary repository of porcelain,
Spin's creations are superb. The pieces
evoke an aesthetic derived from nature;
jars drip with red glaze, and tea and
sake sets bear the patina of ground tofu.
The only things less showy than the
ceramics are the reasonable prices.
6 Fangyuan Xilu, T 6437 8649

Brand New China

The daughter of a diplomat (her mother was Mao Zedong's English teacher), Hung Huang writes a microblog that has 10m followers and oversees fashion magazine *iLook*, which has championed Chinese designers since 1998. She launched this store in 2010 in Sanlitun's glitzy Taikoo Li North shopping mall, using her significant influence to provide a fine platform for the country's rising stars. In this 540 sq m incubation space, the clothing, accessories, furniture and more are displayed on shop fittings that riff off rickshaws and other cultural references. Keep an eye out for Bai Peng's oversized, deconstructed shirts and shawls; angular leather clutches with contrast linings from Hong Kong's Lulu Lam; and bright ceramics by Pilingpalang. *Unit NLG09a, Taikoo Li North, T 6416 9045, www.brandnewchina.cn*

Lost & Found

'Simple furniture inspired by midcentury China' is the tagline of this unique design boutique. Shan Shan, Paul Gelinas and Xiao Mao salvage classic treasures from Beijing's soon-to-be-forgotten recent past, like the discarded Mao-era chairs, and either restore them, or update them as limited-edition pieces. The socialist chic doesn't end there. The brand collaborates with China's oldest functioning thermos factory to produce reissued flasks, and everything from battered leather bags to old-school phones can be found inside the store, which is hidden in a hutong near the Lama Temple. Visiting is like stepping into the world's greatest gift shop dedicated to the Middle Kingdom's modern history, or a communist-inspired Established & Sons. *42 Guozijian Jie, T 6401 1855, www.lostandfound.cn*

ESCAPES

WHERE TO GO IF YOU WANT TO LEAVE TOWN

'He who hasn't climbed the Great Wall is not a real man,' Mao once stated. Avoid touristy Badaling and seek out the more adventurous sections – the Wild Wall sweeps across the north of Greater Beijing and is a two- to three-hour drive away. You'll also find temples and ruins, such as the Royal Mausoleum of Ming, where 13 emperors are interred in a picturesque valley in Changping. There are some delightful places to stay: make a base on Yanqi Lake (opposite), at Brickyard (overleaf), Commune by the Great Wall (see p102) or rent a beautifully renovated farmhouse or barn at the Shan Li Retreats (Miyun, Beizhuang, Huangyankou, T 137 0132 1210), 90km north of Beijing. The bucolic refuge is halfway to Chengde, the escape of the great Qing emperors – it's the Summer Palace on steroids.

Closer to the capital is Xiangshan, an imperial garden at the foot of the Western Mountains, where Beijingers hike, and gape at their smoggy home 25km away. In the hamlet of Chuandixia, further west, villagers live in earth-and-stone dwellings that are 400 years old – a mere instant compared to Zhoukoudian, where history goes back 500,000 years, thanks to the discovery of Peking Man. Keep heading south-west to the 14th-century walled town of Pingyao in Shanxi, which became a banking capital during the Qing dynasty (1644-1912). Stop over at Jing's Residence (16 East Avenue, T 0354 584 1000), a boutique hotel in a 260-year-old merchant's house. *For full addresses, see Resources.*

Sunrise Kempinski, Yanqi Lake

A most unexpected sight by a lake in the lush foothills of the Yanshan Mountains, the 306-room Sunrise Kempinski looks like it got lost en route to another planet. Shanghai Huadu Architect Design Co has covered it in 10,000 shimmering glass panels, and the entrance is shaped like the mouth of a fish, a symbol of prosperity. Interiors by US firm DiLeonardo include a kinetic glass artwork that dominates the lobby, and relaxing rooms with wallpapered panels, printed fabrics and wood floors. Spread over 14 sq km, Kempinski's complex includes the 111-room Yanqi Hotel and 12 boutique hotels on Yanqi Island. Guests can make use of 14 restaurants and bars, two spas, a marina and a nearby watersports centre. The lake is 60km north of Beijing.

18 Jia, Yanshui Lu, Yanqi Lake, Huairou, T 6961 8888, www.kempinski.com

Brickyard, Mutianyu

Jim Spear and Tang Liang bought a house in Mutianyu, in sight of the Great Wall, two decades ago. Since then, the US couple, along with friends Julie Upton-Wang and Peiming Wang, have become involved in the development of the village, culminating in the launch of Brickyard. Formerly a tile factory, it has been transformed into a boutique retreat with a spa, jacuzzi, yoga platform and 25 rooms, each with a huge window facing the mountains. It marries a local aesthetic with repurposed industrial materials (the old kiln chambers are now public spaces) and modern furnishings, dramatic lighting and bright tiles. There is a commitment to sustainability here. Staff are hired from the rural community and a nearby garden supplies the restaurant. *Yingbeigou Village, Huairou, T 6162 6506, www.brickyardatmutianyu.com*

Songzhuang Art Village

The villages north and east of Beijing have proved as important to China's art scene as the French countryside was to the Impressionists. Yet none possess the scale, folklore or staying power of Songzhuang, 30km east of the capital. When this enclave formed in the mid-1990s, anti-establishment figures had to move constantly to dodge the police. But attitudes have changed so much that now the local government sponsors the Songzhuang Art Festival and a museum. Today, around 8,000 artists are based here, and high-profile residents include cynical realists Yue Minjun and Fang Lijun. Its diversions are too numerous to list, but the Artist Village Gallery (pictured, T 6959 8343) is one of the best, with 3,000 sq m of exhibition space set in a large garden.

Commune by the Great Wall

Nestling in rolling forested hills, the 40 villas here were designed by 12 Asia-based architects – standouts are Antonio Ochoa's Cantilever House (pictured) and Kengo Kuma's Bamboo House. The complex has a pool, a tennis court, three restaurants and a path leading to a quiet, unrestored section of the Great Wall. The weekend homes of the new elite are dotted below.
Exit 53, G6 Highway, T 8118 1888

NOTES

SKETCHES AND MEMOS

RESOURCES
CITY GUIDE DIRECTORY

HOTELS
ADDRESSES AND ROOM RATES

Aman at Summer Palace 027
  Room rates:
  double, from RMB3,500;
  Imperial Suite, from RMB28,200
  1 Gongmenqian Jie
  T 5987 9999
  www.amanresorts.com

Brickyard 098
  Room rates:
  double, from RMB1,400
  Yingbeigou Village
  Huairou
  T 6162 6506
  www.brickyardatmutianyu.com

China World Hotel 016
  Room rates:
  double, from RMB2,300
  1 Jianguomenwai Dajie
  T 6505 2266
  www.shangri-la.com

Commune by the Great Wall 102
  Room rates:
  double, from RMB2,200;
  Cantilever House, from RMB2,200;
  Bamboo House, from RMB2,200
  Exit 53
  G6 Highway
  T 8118 1888
  www.commune.com.cn

Hotel Côté Cour 022
  Room rates:
  double, from RMB1,200;
  Superior Suite, from RMB2,000
  70 Yanyue Hutong
  T 6523 9598
  www.hotelcotecourbj.com

EAST 024
  Room rates:
  double, from RMB1,200
  22 Jiuxianqiao Lu
  T 8426 0888
  www.east-beijing.com

The Emperor Forbidden City 017
  Room rates:
  double, from RMB900
  33 Qihelou Jie
  T 6526 5566
  www.theemperor.com.cn

The Emperor Qianmen 017
  Room rates:
  double, from RMB1,500;
  Miracle Suite, from RMB8,800
  87 Xianyukou Jie
  T 6701 7790
  www.theemperor.com.cn

Four Seasons 016
  Room rates:
  double, from RMB3,700
  48 Liangmaqiao Lu
  T 5695 8888
  www.fourseasons.com

Grace 026
  Room rates:
  double, from RMB1,500;
  Grace Suite, RMB2,300
  2 Jiuxianqiao Lu
  798 Art District
  T 6436 1818
  www.gracehotels.com

.The Great Wall Sheraton 016
  Room rates:
  double, from RMB1,000
  10 Dongsanhuan Beilu
  T 6590 5566
  www.sheraton.com.cn

Jing's Residence 096
Room rates:
double, RMB1,400
16 East Avenue
Pingyao
Shanxi
T 035 4584 1000
www.jingsresidence.com

Hotel Kapok 016
Room rates:
double, from RMB800
16 Donghuamen Dajie
T 6525 9988
www.hotel-kapok.com

The Opposite House 030
Room rates:
double, from RMB2,900;
Penthouse, from RMB57,500
11 Sanlitun Lu
T 6417 6688
www.theoppositehouse.com

The Orchid 016
Room rates:
double, from RMB800
65 Baochao Hutong
T 8404 4818
www.theorchidbeijing.com

Park Hyatt 016
Room rates:
double, from RMB2,900
2 Jianguomenwai Dajie
T 8567 1234
www.beijing.park.hyatt.com

Raffles 016
Room rates:
double, from RMB1,800
33 Dongchang'an Jie
T 6526 3388
www.raffles.com

Shan Li Retreats 096
Room rates:
double, from RMB4,500
Miyun
Beizhuang
Huangyankou
T 137 0132 1210
www.shanliretreats.com

Sunrise Kempinski 097
Room rates:
double, from RMB2,300
18 Jia
Yanshui Lu
Yanqi Lake
Huairou
T 6961 8888
www.kempinski.com

The Temple Hotel 020
Room rates:
double, from RMB2,300
23 Shatan Beijie
T 8401 5680
www.thetemplehotel.com

W 016
Room rates:
double, from RMB2,500
2 Jianguomennan Dajie
T 6515 8855
www.starwoodhotels.com

Waldorf Astoria 028
  Room rates:
  double, from RMB3,100;
  Terrace Suite, from RMB5,000;
  Hutong Villa, from RMB20,700
  5-15 Jinyu Hutong
  T 8520 8989
  www.waldorfastoria.com
Yanqi Hotel 097
  Room rates:
  double, from RMB2,900
  18 Jia
  Yanshui Lu
  Yanqi Lake
  Huairou
  T 6961 8888
  www.kempinski.com

WALLPAPER* CITY GUIDES

Executive Editor
Jeremy Case

Associate Editor
Rachael Moloney

Author
Adrian Sandiford

Art Editor
Eriko Shimazaki
Original Design
Loran Stosskopf
Map Illustrator
Russell Bell

Photography Editor
Elisa Merlo
**Assistant Photography
Editor**
Nabil Butt

Sub-Editor
Emily Brooks

Editorial Assistant
Emilee Jane Tombs

Production Controller
Sophie Kullmann

Interns
Pin-Ju Chen
Yijing Li
Alex Shen

Wallpaper* ® is a
registered trademark
of IPC Media Limited

First published 2007
Revised and updated 2011
Third edition 2015

© Phaidon Press Limited

All prices and venue
information are correct at
time of going to press,
but are subject to change.

Contacts
wcg@phaidon.com
@wallpaperguides

More City Guides
www.phaidon.com/travel

Phaidon Press Limited
Regent's Wharf
All Saints Street
London N1 9PA

Phaidon Press Inc
65 Bleecker Street
New York, NY 10012

Phaidon® is a registered
trademark of Phaidon
Press Limited

www.phaidon.com

A CIP Catalogue record for
this book is available from
the British Library.

Printed in China

ISBN 978 0 7148 6844 8

PHOTOGRAPHERS

Iwan Baan
National Stadium,
pp014-015

Eric Gregory Powell
Aman at Summer Palace,
p027
Chairman Mao Memorial
Hall, pp034-035
Duck de Chine, p038
D Lounge, p039
Dali Courtyard, p051
Q Bar, p054
Da Dong, p055
Noodle Bar, p061
Lin Lin, p063
Fei Space, p091
Lost & Found, p095

Lv Hengzhong
Sunrise Kempinski, p097

Tony Law
Hotel Côté Cour,
p022, p023

Robert McLeod
Brickyard, pp098-099

Nathaniel McMahon
Beijing city view,
inside front cover
The Emperor Qianmen,
p017, pp018-019

The Temple Hotel,
p020, p021
EAST, pp024-025
Waldorf Astoria,
p028, p029
Re-Up, p036
Susu, p041
Green T House Living,
pp042-043
Brian McKenna at The
Courtyard, p045
TRB, p046, p047
Okra, pp048-049
Janes & Hooch, p050
Migas, pp052-053
Transit, pp056-057
Moka Bro's, pp058-059
Ichikura, p060
CAFA Art Museum,
pp066-067
400ml, p069, pp070-071
Gao Brothers, p073
Today Art Museum,
pp074-075
Three Shadows
Photography Art Centre,
p076, p077
NAMOC, p078
Pékin Fine Arts, p079
Parkview Green,
pp082-083
Christopher Bu, p090
Brand New China, p094

OJPhotos/Alamy
Temple of Heaven, p033

Pace Gallery
Pace Gallery, p072

Andrew Rowat
CCTV Building, pp010-011

Oak Taylor-Smith
Forbidden City, pp012-013
Hutong, p037
Dongbianmen Watchtower,
pp086-087
Spin Ceramics, pp092-093

Jonathan de Villiers
Linked Hybrid, p081

BEIJING
A COLOUR-CODED GUIDE TO THE HOT 'HOODS

EAST SIDE
Beijing's CBD is rising fast; view the range of glass and steel from the peaceful Ritan Park

UNIVERSITIES
Campus life dominates the north-west, which teems with tech kids and internet cafés

TIANANMEN
Hopscotch through China's past, from the Forbidden City to Chairman Mao's memorial

GULOU
The disappearing hutong still draw the hip crowd to their eateries, bars and boutiques

OLD CITY
Seek out the gems of the emperors' old domain before modernisation swallows them up

SANLITUN
Switching from seedy to swanky, this area remains the heart of Beijing's nightlife scene

For a full description of each neighbourhood, see the Introduction.
Featured venues are colour-coded, according to the district in which they are located.